Kirk,

Beginning with God, I give thanks to him for giving me the most wonderful and loving son. I am truly blessed and inspired by the man that you have become.

You have opened up and shared your thoughts and ideas about your personal experience with family, life, and addiction, which takes courage. In doing so, you are reaching out to so many people who are going through or have gone through some if not all the same issues.

I am very proud of you for wanting to reach out to help others and let them know it's never too late!

Love,
Mom

Praise for *For Your Eyes Only*

"Bondage necessitates freedom, and freedom from the bondage of pornography is certainly hard won. His *f.r.e.e. indeed* process provides deep, authentic, sustainable, and profoundly liberating freedom from the destructive bondage of pornography. Kirk brings a potent blend of significant life experiences, honed wisdom, keen insight, and effective tools to this difficult area that will assist individuals in truly breaking free from the chains of pornography."

—Craig D. Lounsbrough, MDiv, LPC
Licensed Professional Counselor | Certified Professional Life Coach

"I have spent the past ten years helping people daily regain control of their lives from substance abuse. This *f.r.e.e. indeed* program takes the guesswork out of breaking free from pornography. I have known Kirk for over ten years, and he has put together a program I believe could change the lives of many people."

—Tom Roth
Founder, Step Seven Ministries

"Out of the laboratory of his own life and his subsequent walk with Jesus, Kirk Samuels has discovered a proven method of breaking the bondage of pornography in the lives of men which can lead them to freedom. Combining a methodology of mind, body, soul, and spirit, he has helped countless men to freedom and restoration of broken relationships. *For Your Eyes Only* has encapsulated this process so that any man who commits himself to the process can find the freedom he is so desperately looking for. I highly recommend it."

—Larry Russell
Shepherd's Heart Ministry

"Following the six-week training offered by Kirk through the *f.r.e.e. indeed* process has been a great adventure for me. As a former porn consumer, and now as a pastor and counselor, I valued this program for many different reasons: Kirk is very vulnerable in the way he introduces himself and tells you about his story. He puts you at ease immediately and makes you feel totally understood and not judged at all. I like *f.r.e.e. indeed* more than other programs because it approaches the issue of pornography in a very holistic way, taking into consideration every aspect of who you are: mind, soul, and body. It offers simple and very practical solutions and a group of guys to help you with your struggle. What I prefer more than everything is that at the center of every lesson is the encouragement we find in the person of Jesus Christ, who is the solution and the answer to all of our needs as men."

—Eric Dufour
Dufour Ministries

"Pornography is the silent addiction of so many men today. It enslaves men in shame, robs them of their self-worth, and leaves them feeling isolated and alone. Kirk has been there and knows what it's like. He has a passion to see men experience the same freedom he enjoys, and he has a practical plan that works. I highly recommend his class to all men!"

—David Kennedy
Senior Pastor, Newday Seventh Day Adventist Church

FOR YOUR EYES ONLY

The Inside Scoop About Men, *Porn,* and Marriage

KIRK M. SAMUELS

I believe in you
Kianga! Love + Freedom!

Kirk 36

ISBN: 0692950788
ISBN 13: 9780692950784

Library of Congress Control Number: 2017914338
LCCN Imprint Name: Parker, Colorado

Contents

Note to Readers.. *ix*

Acknowledgments .... *xi*

Greeting .... *xiii*

Introduction: The View from the Inside........... *1*

Evolution of Modern Porn Consumption........... *4*

Evolution of Porn Sobriety........................... *8*

My Purpose *11*

Hope for Her Hopelessness.......................... *11*

Sex Addict versus Internet Porn Addict *15*

1 My Story... *19*

2 The Mistress in the Home *29*

Chemistry of the Brain................................ *33*

Mechanics of the Two-Part Addicted Brain....... *34*

3 The Six Vs... *39*

4 (V1) Visualization *41*

5 (V2) Variety *47*

PIED... *49*

6 (V3) Vitality *53*

7 (V4) Victory 57

Availability 58

Submission 59

8 (V5) Vacation 61

Cortisol 62

Oxytocin 62

9 (V6) Validation 65

10 Cycles 69

Addiction Cycle 69

Medicate Cycle 70

What Pain Is He Medicating? 71

Freedom Cycle 72

11 "Just Stop?" 75

Feed the Lion 75

12 IP Mistress Weaknesses 77

Touch 77

Smell 78

Dialogue 79

Her Chivalry 80

The Mistress Spouse 81

To the Guys 85

Epilogue 87

About the Author 89

Note to Readers

It is my intention to provide information leading to inspiration and to open the door for illumination of a difficult topic.

The only reason you are reading this is because God took this broken person with a broken past and made something out of the wreckage. I must begin with giving back to him for being the first to love the unlovable.

There is a reason the first words you read in this book were from my mom. She was the first to show my eyes what unconditional love looks like. I wish I could live up to that. I love you, Mom, and my life is a monument to you and your sacrifice for us. My heart's desire is to lay a foundation for my kids to build their lives upon. I love you four to my life's end and beyond.

To the person suffering from the pain of a trap, I get it. I really get it. You are the reason I write this and do what I do. I want to live an inch wide and a mile deep in my service to others. I care about the individual more than the masses. Keep fighting the battle, and don't focus on losses or failures. The fact that you failed indicates that you are trying. Keep trying, and don't quit until your heart stops.

Acknowledgments

Thank you, Lord. Thank you, Ma and Quentin. The three of us have been through a lot together. We have shared and experienced things no one else would understand. Never have I wavered in my heartfelt belief that you have always had my back. Thanks, Dad, for doing the best you could. I forgive you and hope to see you in heaven. Thanks to Kev, Raj, Terry, Chin, and Seppi for being my crew since Suitland '91. Thanks to Mrs. Betty Scott for being the teacher to pull me out of the chaos that ruled my life back then and putting me in choirs and plays. This is probably the closest I'll get to a Grammy or Oscar speech, and I told you if I had the chance I would thank you. Thanks to the Kennedy family for the stuff I promised I wouldn't share publicly. Thanks to Mike, Brian, Brandon, and Bob for being my phalanx in the beginning of this journey. I wouldn't have made it this far without you guys. Thanks to everyone who contributed to this book. Some wouldn't touch this thing with a ten-foot pole and turned me down, but you all jumped right in with me. I'm glad I didn't decide to do this on my own. Thanks to Dale Steadman for the cover photo and my first professional photo shoot. Thanks to everyone I didn't mention for not being too mad at me. I only get so many words here, people. Thanks to everyone reading this and to everyone fighting the battle. I know you, and you know me. You are my tribe. We are in this together.

Greeting

If you have a husband or significant other caught in the trap of Internet pornography, you are not alone. I hope this is the first resource that was referred to you. Others around you may seem to have it all together—but think again. In this book, you will gain understanding like you've never heard before. This is not meant to make you OK with your partner's habit, but to allow you to look behind the curtain. Women should not have to, and are unable to, compete with today's porn.

I imagine it is hard being a woman today. You are expected to kill the proverbial pig to bring home the bacon. Somehow you must be like the lady on TV who knows fifty different ways to cook up that pig and make it look pretty. Maybe you feel you must meet everyone's needs. Then, when the house is clean, homework is done, bills are paid, kids are bathed and in bed, you must become a porn star in the bedroom . . . every night. You may be frustrated at some point of the journey through this book. In August 2015, *Psychology Today* published an article saying that spouses of people who act out sexually outside the marriage display signs and symptoms of post-traumatic stress disorder. Younger single ladies must somehow get a "pornified" guy's attention and keep the faith that he will see their hearts eventually. Stick with me throughout this book, because there is a method to the madness.

Introduction:
The View from the Inside

Pornography takes you to the loneliest places imaginable. The pain on the inside is matched by very few types of pain on the outside. No one in our society is immune to pornography. It has truly become part of our culture. It moves in like an unwanted roommate and takes over. This roommate moves into your career, your bank account, your relationships, your spiritual life, your church, and anything else you find valuable. Your world view becomes distorted.

Others trying to understand the world of the porn consumer have a distorted view of what is really going on. It's like people looking into a fish tank and thinking they can understand the fish. They may be able to see his world from the outside, but they can never truly know what that world is like. Outsiders cannot fully grasp what it is like to breathe in, move around in, and see everything through that environment. They can walk around the fish tank, while the fish's own understanding is limited by the invisible walls of the tank. When the thermostat malfunctions, they either have no idea how cold and lonely this world becomes or how this world is actually boiling them to death. Outsiders either fail to understand or give up trying to understand, concluding that he should "just stop." What they don't understand is that if he could "just stop," *he would*! He feels that other people don't care how isolated he is.

The same holds true for men struggling with porn consumption. Part of their hopelessness is feeling that even God himself has abandoned them. The consumer doesn't even understand what he is doing. What he wants to do, he doesn't do. The thing he hates doing is exactly what he ends up doing.

If it sounds like I'm being a little dramatic, I am. If it sounds like I'm a little sympathetic, I am. I'm saying what I wish someone would've said at some point along my journey. You will quickly find that I'm not an apologist for the porn-consuming masses. I intend to show you something that no one else has: the point of view of both the imprisoned and the liberated. If more people understood what is going on in the world of a porn consumer, they might view him not through his failures, but through his pain. If more porn consumers understand what is going on beneath the surface, they will see that change is possible and seek proper kinds of medicine for the pain.

> Wisdom is the principal thing;
> Therefore get wisdom.
> And in all your getting, get understanding.
> Exalt her, and she will promote you;
> She will bring you honor, when you embrace her.
> She will place on your head an ornament of grace;
> A crown of glory she will deliver to you.
> **—Proverbs 4:7–9, New King James Version**

Porn statistics, in my opinion, offer mere snapshots of the real picture. No one has ever surveyed me, and I've never met anyone who has participated in a porn survey. As I look at some of the sources of pornography data, I do see some correlation to what I have experienced and have known through the lives of many others I help. Numbers vary, but most males are said to consume pornography on a regular basis. The younger the man's age, the odds of him consuming porn tend to go up significantly. Increasing numbers of females, of all ages, are consuming as well.

Going by the numbers, most marriages end in divorce. When a couple gets divorced, their entire community is affected. Most divorces involve someone with an online sexual stronghold. Young people are increasingly choosing to not even get married. As of the date of this publication, Webroot says that nearly 70 percent of divorces involve infidelity that started online. Nearly 60 percent of divorces involve someone with a porn habit. I would venture to say that porn consumption may be the genesis of most infidelity in our culture.

Pornography is the perfect drug because consumption of it is, for the most part, undetectable to others. Porn is the only drug ever to be free and unlimited. You can literally consume this drug in your sleep. What other drug can that be done with? If cocaine or alcohol were free and unlimited, there would be dead people on every corner. Pornography consumption is easily out of sight and out of our collective moral conscience, whereas you can sit next to a person and see or smell his alcohol or cigarette habit. Today's Internet pornography takes no additional money directly out of your bank account, leaves no smell on your skin or clothes, and cannot be detected with drug testing. Since porn is free and unlimited, there are dead marriages on street corners all around us. If you are wondering why I am categorizing pornography as a drug, stay tuned.

Evolution of Modern Porn Consumption

In the early Internet years, video-store memberships transitioned to paid websites. The Internet made pornography a private endeavor. In the comfort of your own home, you could click a button and have an image load on your personal computer. You could stare at that image as long as you wanted. The availability of broadband Internet in the early twenty-first century was a game changer. It gave everyone access to unlimited quantities of porn—however much they could consume. Surfing for pictures turned into downloading and streaming video. Suddenly, there was no need to go to the video store. No genre or flavor of porn limited your single experience. This allowed people to surf for hours at a time while jumping to any type of porn they can imagine. Any variety of porn was accessible at a moment's notice.

No longer would you have to hide that tape or DVD. Suddenly, the private endeavor could occur even without your wife knowing . . . at least for a while. Data transmission quickly became the bulk of the traffic on our local phone company's networks. Now sites offer free porn, neatly categorized for the consumer. Most middle-aged or older men did not develop a true, deep preoccupation with pornography until free, broad-band porn surfaced.

The modern smartphone not only allows you to have unlimited porn, but now it can be in your pocket! You can surf with broadband speeds from anywhere. Smartphones can use Wi-Fi networks, so you can surf outside coffee shops, schools, restaurants, and churches without affecting your data plan. Pornography is literally floating in the air we breathe and digitally passing through our bodies twenty-four hours a day, whether or not we want it to. The pressure on parents to provide a smartphone for their children means many parents give them to kids as early as elementary school. Parents can monitor data usage over a shared family plan, but there's no easy way to check Wi-Fi usage. Not many parents are savvy enough to check the history or cache on their kid's smartphone. Not many know when their fifteen-year-old has deleted some but not all of that information. This means pornography is the only drug kids can legally bring onto a school campus and share in the lunchroom. What if your twelve-year-old were smoking marijuana on the school bus?

Most males get introduced to porn somewhere between the ages of eight and twelve. Today's elementary schoolers are introduced to the most hardcore and often violent genres. They aren't being introduced to the soft stuff; they are being introduced to the porn equivalent of crack and meth when they go to school. Teens can also share pornographic images of themselves with anyone.

In most places, teens sharing naked or sexual images of

other teens is considered a crime. Conviction could result in your youngster becoming a felon and being registered as a sex offender. In the fall of 2015, news broke of this happening on a large-scale at Cañon City High School in Cañon City, Colorado. Students were using what are called "ghost" apps to store naked or pornographic pictures of other students. In what turned into almost a competition, the collection and exchange of these images went rampant among the students. Once this was discovered, school officials and law enforcement found themselves with a difficult dilemma. This activity qualified as a crime, but how could they possibly arrest and charge hundreds of students? The resulting news story indicated that consideration needed to be given to changing the laws.

In 2015, Cañon City made national news. At least 106 students in the Cañon City School District were reported to be involved in a sexting scandal, but they won't be charged, even though there was "enough evidence to prosecute a handful of students."

"The resulting investigation did not identify any of the potential aggravating factors, such as the involvement of adults, the posting of images through the Internet, coercion or bullying, allegations of unlawful sexual contact and/or retribution or retaliation," Fremont County District Attorney Thom LeDoux said at a press conference Dec. 9.

The distribution, production and possession of sexually explicit material remains a felony.

"We expect that any questionable photographs in existence before this date have been destroyed as required by law," he said. "Law enforcement and the district attorney's office will consider the continued possession of any illegal materials of this nature associated with this situation or otherwise to be an aggravating factor in any future case. In other words, we expect and demand that the children in our community strictly comply with the laws of this state, particularly in this area moving forward."

"The Colorado District Attorney's Council prior to this incident was already working with legislators in an effort to present legislation to the general assembly during the 2016 session that would change the nature of the law, the crime of possession, distribution or creation of sexually exploitative material, which is currently a class three felony," LeDoux said. "There will be a legislative effort in conjunction with the Colorado District Attorney's Council that will take a look at that offense, and I expect will rewrite the offense that said these behaviors will remain crimes in the state of Colorado moving forward."

Bret Meuli, principal at CCHS, said that the nude photographs were in a photo vault app that disguised itself as other applications.

"I was naive," Meuli said. "I had no idea it was out there. Obviously, I'm sure parents trust their kids giving them a cell phone, and even those parents that are checking their cell phones have no clue that they should dig deeper." (*Canon City Daily Record*, 12/31/15)

When crack ran rampant through my hometown of Washington, DC, I don't remember any talk of changing the laws because there were too many people breaking them. Could there be special considerations given for the porn drug because we have quietly conceded to losing this battle?

> *"You never really understand a person until you consider things from his point of view—until you climb into his skin and walk around in it."*
> —**Harper Lee,** *To Kill a Mockingbird*

Evolution of Porn Sobriety

The Foundation for a Drug-Free World says that cocaine, in its natural form of the coca leaf, was found to be used as early as 3000 BC. The Drug Enforcement Administration Museum says that opium, from which heroin and similar drugs are derived, is known to have been used as early as 3400 BC. The Foundation for a Drug-Free World also says that consumption of alcoholic drinks has been found to date to as early as 7000 BC. For someone to say he has been sober from these substances for a long period of time is significant, because these substances have been available from almost the beginning of civilization. Free broadband pornography has existed only for a relative instant in history. Comparing pornography prior to broadband Internet to current pornography is like comparing the potency of cocaine to that of crack—at their foundations they are the same, but the latter is more powerful, cheaper, and more accessible. Therefore it can be difficult for even some professionals to relate to what life is like on broadband pornography. Not many textbooks or long-term studies have been written on the problem's current scale and scope.

These free websites still make a tremendous amount of money. They do this mainly through advertising and the sale of your digital presence online. Statistics say that the sex and porn industry generates more revenue than all professional sports combined! The pornography industry doesn't charge for a seat and sells no food or concessions. Still, tens of billions of dollars are generated annually. Now, the last major barrier to access has come down. No credit card is required. No proof of age or identity is required. No bricks-and-mortar location is necessary. Alas, pornography is free and unlimited at the speed of light around the world. If you think this problem will get better on its own, you are probably high on crack right now.

I am writing from the perspective I know best: a boy and then a man and husband caught in pornography. I wish I could say this is no longer a struggle I wrestle with. Although I no longer consume pornography, I have not forgotten what it was like. What I describe in this book may or may not apply to women who consume pornography. The experience described here may also be applicable to other habits and addictions. My experience may not be the be-all and end-all of what the experience is like.

I am also writing this book because I have been given a new opportunity, and as a result, I must give back. I am a Christian, but I do not consider myself overly "religious." I attend church and am an active member of my church. I don't consider myself anti-porn as much as anti-slavery. By that measure, I'm an abolitionist. I see slavery as a relatively small group of people financially benefiting from the exploitation of trapped masses.

I should not have survived my addiction, and I want to try to help anyone I can, regardless of their spiritual beliefs. As I write this, I am not a pastor, counselor, doctor, or anything of that sort. Most of what I have learned thus far has come from a cemetery, not a seminary. Some may have issues with the fact that I do not have initials after my name and am more practical than clinical. I may even connect dots that others might not. I have learned a great deal from those who are formally educated and seek to work with and tackle this problem with anyone fighting the same battle.

I encourage everyone to seek solid counseling and spiritual help. No one hoping to break the grips of Internet pornography should expect to be able to do it without professional help. I would go so far as to say that professional help is mandatory in the process of getting free.

My Purpose

As a person, surviving this battle has given me purpose in life. It is easier for one to say, "Me too!" than to be the first to put their story out there. A broken stick can draw a straight line, and a pitcher with a hole in it can still pour out what it has left in it. I will be transparent in telling my story, and I will be blunt about what I have learned.

Every porn consumer feels as though he is on an island. Every spouse of a consumer feels the same way. The reality is that if such an island existed, it would be the most populated island on earth. This island would have twice the population of Australia, if it were just filled with American porn consumers. If this includes you, you are not alone. The population of that island suffers in mostly silent frustration.

I am giving a voice to the silent ones and shining light into some dark places. My purpose here is not to provide some deep philosophical or cognitive solutions to the world's porn problem. My purpose here is to help one person understand what someone else's life is like. My purpose is also to help one person understand that he or she is not alone. This may lead some to frustration. Once we begin to truly understand the problem, we can better formulate solutions.

Hope for Her Hopelessness

This is a message I received from a hurting wife. She gave me permission to use it to help you:

Hi, I think my husband and I are getting a divorce. He's been lying to me, hiding porn, acting like he's not accessing it, etc. but I have actually walked in on him "pleasuring" himself twice in the past week. I lost it. I told him to leave and that he's chosen porn and masturbation over his wife and children.

I guess I'm reaching out to you to find out if this is ever effective or if usually men are happy to have the unadulterated time with their phones once they get kicked out.

He blocked me from social media. He's trying to boss me around but I'm not having any of that. HE offended me. Not the other way around. I am so SICK of living this way, being hurt and feeling like I'm competing for him. I don't want it anymore. Anyway, what are your thoughts?

I wished there could've been someone to say he had "been there/done that" when I was there/doing that and needed answers. I was hopeless. Free broadband Internet pornography was not something I had ever heard anyone who experienced dealing with the struggle talk about openly. It is one of the last taboo topics. Everyone around me seemed so damn happy, but my life was falling apart. It seemed as if I were the only husband consuming massive amounts of pornography, with a wife being inadequately comforted by tears on her pillow. Maybe I was the only one feeling as though I had a wife who hated me—not realizing that I hated myself equally as much, if not more. I hope to *be* hope for the woman in relationship with a porn consumer. When I turned to some marriage conferences, other books, spiritual leaders, and mental health professionals, none of them gave practical hope.

I love marriage conferences and have been to many of them. How can a marriage conference be truly effective if as many as half the men in the room are consuming free Internet pornography, ignoring the issues of communication, love, money, or respect? The things we are addressing in these conferences assume a level playing field. In my opinion, most men generally do *not* flock to marriage conferences on their own because the conference is taking them away from who they really are committed to in the home. After the conference, he can never meet his wife's needs for vulnerability and unconditional connection by going back to his habit. He still may expect his wife to try to meet his needs. In this example, both end up hopeless.

I promise this is not a book of rants about how bad the problem is. I'm creating a foundation on which to build. This is meant to show you that you are not alone. Unfortunately, the broader problem only stands to get worse. There is no need for him to let the guilt and shame of this trap keep him from seeking help in getting to the freedom you and your partner both deserve. Most books that are recommended to him merely explain how bad his problem is and that he should stop.

I do not have a morality platform. It is not my intention here to write as a spiritual leader or guide. I'm not here to address what someone should or shouldn't do. Instead, I'm offering hope to those hurting from a problem I understand very well. I'm a subject-matter expert and want to share the wisdom I have gained. The fact that he struggles with Internet pornography indicates that something inside of him is not satisfied with present circumstances. If he were fine with consumption, pornography would not be a "problem" in his life. I'm not going to pat him on the back, rub his belly, and tell him everything is OK. There is a life greater than you've ever known beyond the chains of bondage. Life will still have its ups and downs, but you can face the pain of life without *his* medication. You know as well as I do *that* medication sucks! It's hopeless cutting of the soul by using something that causes pain to replace another pain.

I surely don't consider myself as perfect. I'm a wounded warrior from this battlefield and will most likely continue to walk with a limp because of my battle scars. There are many smart people with YouTube videos or articles posted online about the information in this book. I have found bits and pieces of information in this way. Through my searching, I have not found anyone who put these pieces of information together to relate them to pornography. I will continue to constantly look for that next piece of the puzzle and bring it to you.

I hope to inspire new fields of study concerning the effects of Internet pornography. I hope to give you a perspective you may not have known previously. This ain't your grandfather's or even your father's type of porn problem. I hope the perspective I can provide from the inside will help marriage conference organizers include new information to attendees. I hope other authors will stretch the boundaries of what has become the common approach to reaching the porn consumer and their spouse. I hope spiritual leaders will see that it's not as easy to stop the downward spiral we see in the homes of those they lead. Today's pornography can become a holistic problem. Holistic problems require holistic solutions. I hope the woman struggling with the presence of pornography in her relationship can feel encouraged that there is a sweet melody beyond the deafening silence of her hopelessness. I hope his eyes will only be reserved for you.

Sex Addict versus Internet Porn Addict

Is your man an addict? There are many definitions of addiction. I resonate with a definition by Dr. Gabor Mate. I'm not in the position to qualify every part of his medical and counseling philosophy or perspective. Loosely described, his definition is that addiction consists of satisfying a craving with something that provides only temporary relief, resulting in negative consequences. By that criteria, I was an addict! As a matter of fact, most of us are or have been addicted to something.

Another source of frustration for the porn consumer is being tagged as a "sex addict." They are not the same thing. Let me illustrate with this example: I have one biological brother. We have the same mother and father and the same last name. We are in the same family. Some might say we look alike, though I tend to think I'm much better looking than him. If we were both in the same room and someone yelled, "Samuels!" we might both turn to look. If that same person yelled, "Kirk!" odds are my brother would not look to see if that person was calling him. If you were talking to him and kept calling him "Kirk," he would probably grow frustrated and eventually tell you that is not his name or begin tuning you out.

This is like the porn addict. Even if by Dr. Mate's definition he is an addict, calling him a sex addict will not reach him. Granted, the two types of addiction might be in the same family and share the same pathology. I've even had a well-known person in the anti-porn industry tell me, "Sex addict . . . porn addict . . . same guy." That was a shock to me, because this guy has written several books on the topic.

The porn addict will not truly respond to being called a sex addict. He says, "How can I be a sex addict if I'm not even having sex?" He believes part of his problem is that he is not actually having sex. Additionally, he sees sex addicts as the people who stroll red-light districts or engage in other illicit sexual activity to scratch their itch. How can we expect the eleven-year-old porn addict to respond to being called a sex addict if he's never seen a naked woman in real life?

A good friend of mine tells me the story of going to see a counselor about the porn use that was controlling his life. The counselor told my friend not much could be done for him. This counselor specialized in clients who were spending copious amounts of money on prostitutes or venturing into illegal activity. You can imagine how my friend felt upon leaving the counseling office that day. In some cases, the porn addict is in fact a sex addict acting out within the bounds of pornography. Mental health professionals will have to somehow define that situation. I'm trying to tell you what *the consumers* are thinking. Ideally, we can begin to understand that sometimes porn addiction needs to be looked at and treated differently than any other addiction. Finally, the fact that he consumes or has consumed porn does not mean that he is of imminent danger to anyone else in terms of acting out.

My Story

MY STORY begins in a cemetery outside of Washington, DC.

My dad was a Vietnam War veteran. He met my mom, who worked for a phone company, after returning home as a retired, 100 percent disabled Marine. I have learned that he had another son prior to me, in California. I recently discovered he had a daughter—my sister—that we had no idea about. He suffered from post-traumatic stress disorder. My earliest memories include visiting him in St. Elizabeth's Mental Hospital. Back then, I did not know he was a recovering drug and alcohol addict. Later in life, I heard him mention something about getting arrested for rape. I would be forty-one years old before I confirmed with my mother that what I remembered him saying was true.

My parents were married seven months before I was born. My mom and I first lived with my grandmother and great-grandmother in northeast DC. When it was time for me to go to public school, my mom moved us to an apartment in the Maryland suburbs. This was where I lived for my first seven years of public school. My neighborhood friends grew to be the source of my male identity. I hung out with a crew of mostly older boys who had no steady male presence in the home either.

My elementary school was in the neighborhood bordering College Park, Maryland. You could not have two more different worlds. My school friends all lived in huge houses with parents who were lawyers, doctors, career police officers, and business owners. Everyone had dads at home and, mostly, moms who worked in the home. The first time I sat down for an actual two-parent family dinner was with the Goldstein family. I had to ask my mother afterward what a brisket was and was it part of a pig. For us, a "family dinner" was when everyone who branched out from my great-grandmother would get together, normally during a holiday. The dinner would almost always include some part of a pig.

In first grade, I would come home after school and let myself in with the key that hung around my neck on a shoe-string. I would later learn of the term "latchkey kid." Once home, I kept myself busy mainly by watching television. When my mom got home, we would eat and call it a night. This was our basic routine with very little change. I leaned heavily on my neighborhood friends to teach me life lessons.

When my father was home from the mental hospital, things at home would either be good or really bad. Walking in the door, I never knew what father I would get. It never took long to figure it out though. My brother was born around the time I was in first grade. I went to an afterschool babysitter in second grade, but I was back to the key from third grade on. I told everyone my father was in the Marines; no way could I tell anyone he was in a mental hospital. When he was in the mental hospital, I had to learn the art of repeated separation. When he was home for brief stints, there was abuse of nearly every type in the home.

The most impactful lesson my neighborhood crew taught me came one day when I was in third grade. Knowing I was home alone, they decided to hang out at my apartment after school. One of them brought over the pornographic video *Behind the Green Door*, which would change my life forever and bring me to writing this book. More than thirty years later, I can recall that day. It wasn't a lesson I was ready for nor one I expected to learn. I could only sit and watch in silence. I knew

I wanted *that*, what I saw on the screen, as much and as long as I could get it. I know now the brain explosion that took place literally altered my brain, even to this day. That was when my subconscious learned that pain I introduced from the outside could medicate the pain I could not control on the inside.

My quest to keep getting that next hit seemed to drive my better judgment into the ditch for the next three decades of my life. I went through the school years driven mostly by the quantity of girls I could get to try to fill that growing void in my soul. I lost my actual virginity when I was fifteen to a twenty-nine-year-old. I thought it was cool and could not wait to tell all my friends about it. Looking back, I know now the act was illegal.

College opened a new playground for me. I had access to what seemed like exponentially more females of every variety. For the first time, I was earning excellent grades and loved the freedom. For short periods of time, I seemed to have a grip on the void I would normally be trying to fill.

The one constant that carried me through high school and college was my inability to have a successful relationship with a girlfriend. Through no fault of their own, I always seemed to find a way to suddenly dump them for someone new. My guilt would haunt me. I could not seem to commit. I knew hearts were broken, and to this day, I regret those sad scenes. None of the women knew about my secret struggle. I hated the way I viewed relationships and now understand that I was unable to maintain emotional or relationship connections with any of these women.

Throughout high school, I knew I wanted to be a Coast Guard helicopter pilot. After two years of doing well in college, I was a lock for an officer scholarship program. I had made it; a full scholarship for my last two years of school plus an active-duty paycheck meant I was a big deal on campus. I had a car and an apartment. I was also in great physical shape. I had a guaranteed future as a Coast Guard officer. It was all coming together.

To keep myself busy, I worked part-time at a men's clothing store. The men's store was attached to a women's store. A few months before I was to graduate college, I saw a new face at the store. She became my new girlfriend. It was a rocky road, to say the least. I graduated in four years with about forty extra credit hours. Officer Candidate School (OCS) was not difficult for me. It was also very close to my college, so I kept in touch with my girlfriend. As I neared the end of OCS, my girlfriend revealed to me that she was pregnant. The only right thing for any guy to do if he did not want to be like his dad was to propose, right?

After graduation from OCS, I was sent to a ship in Key West, Florida. My girlfriend and I married six months later. Just before the wedding, she relayed news from my mom that my father had died. He died alone in a chair while living at someone's house. The last time I remember seeing him was when he was around forty years old, and I was finishing high school. His death hit me in kind of a numb place. I had always hoped that one day things between us would be reconciled, and he would tell me who I was as a man. My thoughts at the time were that he could not even stick around long enough to give me validation or see that I could still become a good man and a good father. Now I would have to go forward with never being given that identity and having to break through the forest alone.

The wedding was exactly seven days after his funeral. In one week, I went from crying at my father's graveside service in my blue uniform to standing in my white uniform watching my six-month-pregnant bride walk down the aisle. My first daughter was born three months later. Everything seemed so complete. If only I had a clue as to who I was supposed to be in my home.

I excelled onboard the ship. It didn't help that I related more with many of the young (and especially minority) members of the crew than I did with the other officers. This was a definite no-no in terms of etiquette. The fatal snare for my career was that females could serve onboard ships. Even though I had been accepted to and was departing shortly for flight school, my career was cut short due to my weakness.

We moved from Key West to Denver, Colorado, when I accepted a job with the local phone company. By now, there was another daughter on the way, and she was born shortly after we moved. As much as I tried to convince myself that everything was about to turn around, my late-night web surfing as well as other unresolved issues between my wife and me led to separation and eventual divorce.

Newly single and completely broken, was a valley that left me with little hope. I was lonelier than I had ever been. My life was pitiful. The only thing left to do was get a second job waiting tables—and of course drowning my sorrows in anything that I could. The passing months looked like years.

A coworker introduced me to a woman at the office. We hit it off right away and went from zero to sixty in no time. We were inseparable, and her family embraced me. I wouldn't be talking about her if we hadn't gotten married. Blending in the family was difficult, to say the least. Difficulties with my daughters were just the beginning of things we had to overcome. After being together for a couple of years, she told me she was pregnant. I had been laid off and had no money. Things between us became more turbulent. Six months into the pregnancy, she walked in on me cheating on her. Feel free to insert every dastardly name you can about me. That rocked everything. We sought help from pastors, counselors, and whoever else we could. She stayed with me, and we were married three months after our daughter was born.

After several years, we adopted a son and settled into a great house in a great neighborhood. My older daughters were moving into their teen years, and we still had issues blending as a family. Pressure mounted, and life got harder to manage. I was less capable of hiding my demons and struggles from my wife. I discovered free porn, and it quickly took over my life.

The years were passing, and I saw my life going full-speed toward the brick wall of my fortieth birthday. I always associated that number with my father's last major birthday before he died, when I saw him for the last time until he lay in a casket at the ripe old age of forty-six. I never wanted to turn forty and was afraid of it. My bondage had taken its toll on me, and the weight of it over the years had worn my soul down into submission. I saw a way to rid myself of the demon. The night before my thirty-ninth birthday, I led all four of my kids in prayer to accept Jesus into their life. The next few days were all about preparation of my resolve.

That next weekend, I told my wife I was going to hang out with some old friends. When that Saturday night came, I packed my computer and my Smith & Wesson .40 caliber and said good-bye to her and the kids. I checked into a cheap hotel and loaded one round in the magazine. I logged in to Facebook to type a good-bye message. I was still getting "happy birthday" posts. One of the first posts was from my brother—not to me, but about something random. I thought about the night my father was straddling my mother's back as he punched her. I was just a young teenager, but I jumped on his back and grabbed his arm while yelling at him to look at my brother. I overheard my father telling my mom one night that before he died, he would kill her and her "punk son" (me). Those words still haunt me when I try to go to sleep at night. I knew he loved my brother, so I guessed looking at him might put some sense into my father. It did.

That moment at the computer though, I went from that memory to an image of my son, who had already experienced so much loss in his life. I pictured him yelling for his dad to not leave him. I dissolved into deep painful sobbing and hatred of myself and the world.

I had a problem though. The monster was still hungry. My

pain called out to me stronger than ever. Normal porn surfing would not be enough. I began a quest to find someone—anyone—who would come to my room and be the outlet for the pain. It didn't take long. There are a lot of people with the same vices roaming the Net at those hours.

Several hours later, at daybreak, I left the room and headed home to what I knew would be more hell. I got home to hours of yelling and screaming and then found myself on the way to the pastor's house. This is where I would stay off and on over the next couple of weeks. My wife and I began seeing a new counselor and worked out a plan to stay at our house on different nights. I grew to hate the feeling of imposing on the pastor's family. They took better care of me than I did of myself. I didn't tell them, but I started to sleep in the back of my truck on the nights I did not stay at their house. I would bathe in my company's bathroom early in the morning before anyone got there. Those were character-building nights.

I was serving as a greeter at church on the weekends, and no one knew I was sleeping in my truck in a hospital parking lot. One of those nights, I began to formulate a plan to drive to the emergency room entrance, then call them on the phone and tell them to come get me. When I saw them walking out the door, I would kill myself and hope they could donate my organs.

That night, I had a conversation with God. I told God that either he hated me and never wanted me free from this, or he would wake me up the next morning and *show* me how to get free. He began to show me, and I in turn began to teach people the practical plan I developed to get free. I started teaching the class out of the same hospital I used to park and sleep at. After years of teaching this formula, others began experiencing freedom for the first time.

Ironically, my second marriage ended after I got free from porn and I began to live my purpose. You will have to wait for my next book to explain this dynamic.

I hope my story inspires strong feelings in you, whether good or bad. I am not writing from a place of zero temptation. You cannot have something dominate your life for three decades and expect to walk away quickly and easily. I turned my test into my testimony. I now have a story to tell and experience to draw from. I have achieved a freedom from porn that I once thought was impossible. I teach specific strategies to offensively fight the battle with free broadband pornography.

I told you my story so that maybe you can identify with some part of it. I know that some will judge me, and I may even lose some friends and face criticism. I care more about you than people who will judge me. Telling my story was my way of having some skin in the game. Maybe you can see that you are not alone. I am willing to put my garbage on the curb for all to see because I believe many will read my story and say, "Wow, me too." Those people are the reason I write this book. I don't have advanced degrees, a counseling practice, or any big claim to fame. Sometimes our pain is our platform.

2

The Mistress in the Home

PORN BRINGS a mistress into the home. That image might seem extreme, but this is the case when someone has a female-consuming porn habit. The reverse could apply if the porn consumed is that of men, but by far, most porn viewing involves a female as a commodity.

A mistress is commonly thought of as a woman "on the side" to whom the husband goes to for what he does not receive in the home. This mistress seems to easily understand and meet his needs. His wife wishes he would think about her as much as he thinks about the mistress. Men can compartmentalize. To him, having a mistress is just another room in the office building of his life. He probably loves his wife and kids. He often justifies his choice to consume porn because having the outlet helps him maintain the front he puts on. He gets to live his manhood dream of dinner at the table with the family and the boyhood dream of excitement—as well as intense sex, of course. Sometimes he even closes his eyes and thinks about the mistress during times he's having sex with his wife. Ouch!—too soon?

This porn type of "intimacy" is cheap and easily consumed. This type of "intimacy" makes true intimacy a spectator sport. The adulterous relationship is a transaction. Both parties get to feel needed and wanted by someone. What starts out as a little bit of time together will consume more and more of the man's schedule. When they are not together, they think about each other and look for the next opportunity to see each other. He knows it's wrong, but he is torn between the one he loves and the one he feels more committed to.

All of you should get out of my head and pay attention, because a setup is coming.

When today's porn attaches to your family, it is like another woman has attached herself to the home. This mistress is a third party to, but also clearly *in*, the marriage. "IP," or Internet Protocol, is the method of using an Internet address to send and receive data. The IP Mistress lives *in* the family's home. She even has her own room—the room where he spends time with her for hours on end. He doesn't even do that for his wife.

The fact that he has this mistress indicates he's trying to fill a hole. This is definitely a God-sized hole. The IP Mistress is free in a couple of ways. Not only is there no out-of-pocket expense, but she is *always* available for him. What she will do for him is unlimited. There is no line she will not cross. She never says no, and he never experiences rejection from her. She never argues with him. When they have a short disruption in their relationship, she quickly forgives him and welcomes him back. She's always in the mood. She can be any age, race, height, weight, or have any hair color, and can change at his will from minute to minute. She has a flawless, even if surgically enhanced, appearance. She never has a headache. She never has a cold and never tells him anything negative—unless he wants her to. She provides him with more excitement and "passion" than he can handle. Variety is her specialty. She can become anyone he sees throughout the day. The boy in him and the man in him can be validated and affirmed at the same time. She is his loudest cheerleader. She tells him, "Yes. You are good. You are the best. I will be happy with whatever you do. I will give you whatever it is you need from me. I will sacrifice my body for your deepest needs."

In a weird way, these also sound like things a mother or even God would say. His heart perceives this aspect of the mistress as deep intimacy, and as a result, he forms a deep connection with her. She gets so deep into his mind that he can even be with the IP Mistress in his sleep! What other drug can people consume in their sleep?

The IP Mistress has a monopoly in our homes, families, and society. She has achieved this status by only asking how she can better serve and meet his sexual needs. He has more than one need, but that is all she seeks to satisfy. We must look at the evidence that the IP Mistress is virtual and cannot exist outside of a 2-D or 3-D image. Somehow, she has tapped into the deepest need of millions of men. Since she cannot physically touch him or vice versa, it is clear she is meeting some deeper need.

The IP Mistress is jealous and becomes very controlling. She demands all his attention. He subconsciously counts the minutes, hours, or days until he sees her again. She can take so much from him sexually that he has very little if anything left for his wife. She can cause him to need a pill to be sexual with his wife. He does not need a pill to be with her. This mistress offers him an escape from the harsh realities of manhood. With her, he can relax and be himself with no judgment. He is always seeking a better experience and visits her often. His post-encounter guilt creates a cycle of consumption that keeps him coming back to her. He can go to a secluded island with her. She doesn't tell him that she will leave him on that island, feeling increasingly lonely as time goes on. Sometimes he will visit the IP Mistress when he's feeling angry, hurt, or rejected by the woman in his life.

I'll remind you that the only thing God said wasn't good during the creation week was man's solitude. He said this although he, God, was with the man, and the woman was inside him. This was when God pulled the woman out of man. There is so much of the IP Mistress available that her presence shows up in other areas of his life. It can show up when others are introduced to her through him. A son, daughter, or relative can be introduced to pornography through his evidence they would find. The IP Mistress wants to be in everyone's life. This is often very easy for her to achieve, because kids are given Internet-capable electronic devices at a young age.

A human cannot keep up nor compete with an IP Mistress. No human should try to attempt being what the IP Mistress is. It is impossible. The IP Mistress is not one person. She is a factory, producing an unlimited and free supply to be consumed. She is primarily produced by men, so she knows the soul of a man very well. The past, present, or future wife can never compete with this mistress.

If this is hard or frustrating for you to read, imagine how a man feels when someone tells him to "just stop." Being reminded of his struggle or last failure can be equally frustrating. Quitting a real-life mistress would be infinitely easier than quitting the IP Mistress.

At some point, his online obsession extends off the screen and into the real world. This is why most divorce cases involve Internet pornography. The wife or girlfriend knows the IP Mistress is in the home and can feel her presence when she walks in. The mistress is always in the room.

I can recall standing in a line for concessions at a Christian concert. Two younger women were standing behind me. One was consoling the other concerning a boyfriend or husband's porn consumption. I wondered if he was at the concert or at home—consuming porn.

Chemistry of the Brain

The things that trap us are not specifically what we get addicted to. Whether it is food, cigarettes, spending, debt, work, drugs, gambling, sex, or pornography, these things feed our craving for a chemical release. Brain cells, called neurons, communicate with each other using chemicals called neurotransmitters. They mostly fall into the category of either excitatory or inhibitory. Two of these neurotransmitters are dopamine and serotonin. Dopamine is excitatory, while sero-tonin is inhibitory. Dopamine is a natural body chemical that is like a gas pedal. It floods your brain's engine with the fuel to drive you to certain goals or feelings. Serotonin is a natural body chemical that is like a brake pedal to slow you down. Dopamine drives you to want that sweet chocolate dessert, while serotonin, triggered by tryptophan, makes you sleepy after you eat turkey. Have you ever wondered why trying to quit something immediately is called going "cold turkey"?

WebMD describes serotonin like this: "Serotonin is a chemical produced by the body that enables brain cells and other nervous system cells to communicate with one another. Too little serotonin in the brain is thought to play a role in de-pression. Too much, however, can lead to excessive nerve cell activity, causing a potentially deadly collection of symptoms known as serotonin syndrome." When you have a problem with serotonin levels, you tend to require meds like Prozac or Zoloft to help treat the signs of depression. Internet-porn bondage has a lot more to do with the balance between these two chemicals than you realize.

Mechanics of the Two-Part Addicted Brain

The National Center for Biotechnology Information esti-mates that your brain has up to one hundred billion neurons. Estimates say there are 0.15 quadrillion neuron connections in the brain. Those connections are called synapses. Continual and repeated passing of these signals is how stronger pathways are created and addictions are born. Most have heard about the conscious and subconscious mind. Let's think of the brain in two parts from the ground up. At the core is a group of structures called the limbic system. This is the first part of the brain to fully develop. Its main job is to keep us alive. How it does this is primarily by motivating us to certain behavior. We need to do things like eat, rest, and—yes—have sex. We also need to avoid pain. This part of the brain works almost invisibly, beneath the surface. Telling him to "just stop" only intensifies the limbic system and causes a greater short-term struggle. I believe most addiction treatments or sobriety methodologies focus mostly on weakening the limbic system.

I have heard men tell me they needed to pray about my offer to help them get free from porn. Do you really need to pray about that, bro? If a man must contemplate the notion of getting free by involving God in the discussion, his wife has no chance! I rarely hear back from that guy. At this point, I only want to work with people who are desperate to get free or help others do so.

The limbic system is also referred to as the "reward center" of your brain. To seek pleasure or avoid pain, the limbic system can hit the dopamine gas pedal to stimulate a craving for the desired reward. It is looking for the payoff in life. Spouses should feed into the deep payoffs that stimulate their mate. When you know what motivates your partner, pressing the dopamine gas pedal toward that reward is essential. Reward them with that thing they crave. It's not always purely sexual, though often sex is the conduit through which his true need is received. Once porn consumption is firmly locked in, every minute without the IP Mistress can make him feel as if he is suffocating.

> *"As you peel back the layers from the behavior, people are feeling the loneliness inside. Oftentimes as that need gets pinged, it's a profound core-level response inside of people. That's why it overrides their frontal lobe."*
> —**Harvey Powers, PhD, Founder, Redimere Group**

Higher-level reasoning resides in your prefrontal cortex. This is where logic, morals, and what we call our conscience exist. The limbic system might be the gas pedal, but the prefrontal cortex is the steering wheel. Motivations exist on a primal level, but where those motivations are directed resides up top.

The limbic system has more time in the sandbox than the prefrontal cortex. We come out of the womb knowing to eat, poop, and cry for what we need. The limbic system is strong, really strong. When there is inner pain, often early in life, and we experience something that even temporarily meets our need, an "arousal template" is created. These pathways can be so engrained that a scan can show what appear to be pockets in the brain. The prefrontal cortex can see the consequences and hope for better. The two brain parts are locked in a battle.

Thus forms the addiction, meeting Dr. Mate's definition of unsuccessfully satisfying cravings with negative consequences. The addiction cycle kicks in because your brain desensitizes itself to the high levels of dopamine and other chemicals. You can never recreate that first high.

In 2014 the *Journal of American Medical Association* (JAMA) published an article linking high volumes of pornography consumption with the visible altering of the human brain's structure.

As if that isn't enough, other substances come into play within this battle. Stimulants like amphetamines flood the brain with dopamine. This is like holding down that gas pedal to go as fast and as far as the fuel will allow—but immediately. Opiates include heroin, morphine, OxyContin, and Vicodin. In the brain, they look and act like endorphins that are released with exercise as well as the feeling of love and connection, but in a stronger way. The brain loves this immensely, so buckle your seatbelt for the ride.

DeltaFosB is a brain protein that has been linked to all kinds of addiction. Once this switch is turned on, the drive to continue seeking relief of the craving is locked in. Even when the consumer stops the addictive activity, DeltaFosB can remain in the system for up to six to eight weeks. Because it is a sexual outlet, porn consumption stimulates dopamine, endorphins, and DeltaFosB.

3

The Six Vs

THE IP Mistress is a friend with real benefits to his life. This causes him to grow deeply connected to her. He welcomes her into his dark, insecure places because he trusts her. She has proven herself trustworthy. She does this by repeatedly giving him visualization, variety, vitality, victory, vacation, and validation. These six Vs are seen in "www"—the abbreviation for "world wide web" that precedes web addresses.

We can peek behind the curtain of the male spirit to see what makes him so loyal and committed to the IP Mistress. If he consistently receives these six Vs from any woman, especially without asking, his attraction will become commitment. His commitment will turn into deep loyalty. His deep loyalty will create dependency. The IP Mistress understands how powerful his sexuality is. Her six Vs capture his mind, body, and soul purely through his sexuality. She doesn't provide financially, and she doesn't cook or clean for him. The only question the IP Mistress asks is, "How can I satisfy you sexually?"

4

Visualization

"The eyes are the windows to the soul."
—Proverb

IT TAKES approximately three to four hundred milliseconds to blink your eyes. A sexually suggestive image registers in the brain in under thirteen milliseconds. Men, in particular, are visually dominated creatures. The IP Mistress knows a man better than he might know himself. She understands how he is wired and exploits that information. She always provides him a visual buffet. This drug is consumed through the eyes.

She begins by appealing to his eyes with her looks. This is where we find the dopamine spike. Since dopamine is the gas pedal of the brain, these spikes are why drugs like cocaine and meth are so addictive. Increased dopamine is also an effect of prescription medications like Adderall and Ritalin. He may be self-medicating diagnosed or undiagnosed attention

deficit disorder/attention deficit hyperactivity disorder (ADD/
ADHD).

> The hallmark symptoms of ADD are easy distract-
> ibility, impulsivity, and sometimes, but not always
> hyperactivity or excess energy. These people are
> the on the go. Type A personalities. Thrill seekers.
> High-energy-, action oriented-, bottom line-, gotta-
> run-type people. They have lots of projects going
> simultaneously. They're always scrambling. They
> procrastinate a lot and have trouble finishing things.
> Their moods can be quite unstable, going from high
> to low in the bat of an eye for no apparent reason.
> They can be irritable, even rageful, especially when
> interrupted or when making transitions. Their
> memories are porous. They daydream a lot. They
> love high-stimulus situations. They love action and
> novelty. Just as this kind of problem can get in the
> way at work, it can also interfere with close relation-
> ships. Your girlfriend can get the wrong impression
> if you're constantly tuning out or going for fast
> action. (Hallowell and Ratey, *Driven to Distraction*
> [Anchor Books, 1994])

In doing research for this book, I realized that I have had
every sign of ADD for as long as I can remember. Among
other challenges, I have hated not being able to focus on
much, if anything, and I read my first book cover to cover only

at the age of thirty-five. The only time I felt peace within the mental chaos was when I was with the IP Mistress. Unlike with most human relationships, she calmed my mental noise and never ridiculed me for my bad grades in school or for being forgetful. As a matter of fact, she made allowances for my inability to focus. When I discovered broadband-Internet porn, I would commonly have six to eight different browsers open at one time, all evenly spaced out on my screen, with a different scene playing on each. Most of my daydreaming was about my IP Mistress. Without her dopamine spikes, it was extremely difficult to get through days when the volume was high on the mental noise or when I had many things going on in my mind.

> *"The escalation of pornography comes in just like it does with cocaine where you escalate the dosage chasing that first high. This is where the perversion within pornography shows up."*
> —Chris J. West, MA, DO, ABAARM

The IP Mistress spends time preparing for her encounter with your man. She has professional hair and makeup, just like many brides on their wedding day. Her clothing highlights the parts of her he is most stimulated by. She wears clothes or lingerie that stimulate his visual cortex. Over time, she doesn't wear larger underwear. She might wear shoes that make her legs take on a sexier shape. All this is purely for his viewing pleasure. The IP Mistress never wears the same outfit twice. Her makeup never fades and almost seems as if it is reapplied without him noticing during their encounter.

Since the IP Mistress knows he is a visual creature, she has sex with him in ways that take his viewpoint into consideration. She never hesitates to show her body. She knows he will become more visually attracted to her because she continually reveals herself to him. She is sure to show him everything that is available to him. All-you-can-eat restaurants have learned from her: no need to look at the menu when you can just walk up and down the buffet. She maintains eye contact whenever possible. The lights are always on. Porn is produced with the camera view as the priority. If it is not captured in the lens, it doesn't count. Porn sex normally happens in positions that do not consider the female's enjoyment.

His relationship with the IP Mistress creates a Pavlovian response. He becomes conditioned to look at all females through the lens of the porn camera. The way some women dress today makes it more difficult for him to go without this stimulation.

Schoolgirls used to compete with popular girls in school; now they must compete with paid porn actresses. Now boys as young as ten and eleven years old are asking girls in their class for sex and sex acts they say aren't considered actual sex.

Sometimes the hardest place for him to be free from this cycle is in church. Women may or may not realize that they can cause a brother to stumble with what they wear. I'm not trying to Puritanize women's fashion, but many men have struggled because of the worship leader's short or tight clothing. Men's brains can lock images strongly into the deepest regions. These images can be recalled and played back on demand at any time.

The sexual brain generally starts as a blank slate. If a man and woman have their first sexual experience on their wedding night, the only baseline they have is each other. In our culture, unless a young person is kept in a closet and never let out of the house, there is no way to escape seeing sexually suggestive images. Whether they are regular porn consumers or not, most men can recall their first exposure. If this exposure resulted in a neurological Big Bang, he will probably be hooked for decades if not the rest of his life. Many men were exposed but not hooked. I have found that if first exposure occurs after age thirteen, the guy is less likely to be hooked for life.

His eyes should only be for the real woman in his life.

5

Variety

"Variety is the spice of life."
—**William Cowper, "The Task"**

THE ONLY thing better than something fantastic to look at is a lot of fantastic things to look at. The IP Mistress provides an unrealistic amount of variety. The male brain is wired to get excited by variety and particularly sexual variety. A phenomenon known as the Coolidge Effect was first explained by animal behavior specialist Frank Beach in 1955. The theory is that male (and some female) mammals seem able to be quickly and repeatedly aroused when presented with a vast selection of available mates.

The IP Mistress provides endless variety. Her variety gives your man an extra boost of dopamine. She spices up a predictable life. As a reminder, she can be any age, race, height, weight, or hair color and can change from minute to minute.

She role-plays with him. She also provides him a variety of sexual experiences. She is a sexual chameleon with enough variants that he will never see them all. Ironically, his IP Mistress provides continual variety while being completely predictable in her ability to do so. He knows exactly where to find her and literally how to push her buttons.

> Traditional factors that once explained men's sexual difficulties appear insufficient to account for the sharp rise in erectile dysfunction, delayed ejaculation, decreased sexual satisfaction, and diminished libido during partnered sex in men under 40. This review (1) considers data from multiple domains, e.g., clinical, biological (addiction/urology), psychological (sexual conditioning), sociological and (2) presents a series of clinical reports, all with the aim of proposing a possible direction for future research of this phenomenon. Alterations to the brain's motivational system are explored as a possible etiology underlying pornography-related sexual dysfunctions. This review also considers evidence that Internet pornography's unique properties (limitless novelty, potential for easy escalation to more extreme material, video format, etc.) may be potent enough to condition sexual arousal to aspects of Internet pornography use that do not readily transition to real-life partners, such that sex with desired partners may not register as meeting expectations and arousal

declines. Clinical reports suggest that terminating Internet pornography use is sometimes sufficient to reverse negative effects, underscoring the need for extensive investigation using methodologies that have subjects remove the variable of Internet pornography use. In the interim, a simple diagnostic protocol for assessing patients with porn-induced sexual dysfunction is put forth. (National Center for Biotechnology Information, Aug 5, 2016)

PIED

Porn-induced erectile dysfunction (PIED) is a condition credited to excessive consumption of broadband pornography. A male can consume so much pornography that he is no longer able to be aroused by a real human being. Ironically, the only cure for PIED is broadband pornography! This is tied heavily to the variety factor as well as the mechanical stimulation of masturbation. A physically mature male can regain normal function after prolonged abstinence from pornography. But a developing brain can never learn what it is like to be aroused by human interaction; therefore a young male developing PIED may never be able to gain natural functionality.

The porn consumer's issues may include some degree of clinical-attachment disorder. Never having to commit is part of the novelty of the IP Mistress. She seems to always know what he likes and to want the same thing. Over time, he will need to consume more violent or unnatural types of sex to achieve the same level of arousal.

Consuming more violent or unnatural types of sex can cost lives. On October 5, 2012, ten-year-old Jessica Ridgeway woke herself up. She had plans to walk to school with a friend, but she never made it. No one knew that seventeen-year-old Austin Sigg was sitting in his vehicle nearby. Austin had unsuccessfully tried to snatch a female jogger previously and decided this day that he would take any female smaller than him. Jessica would never be seen alive again. There are many specific details of the case that police have not released. What has been made public is that Sigg kidnapped and sexually assaulted Jessica Ridgeway before he killed her. Parts of her body were found in a field, and the rest of Jessica's body was in the crawl space of his mother's home.

Sigg was sentenced to life plus eighty-six years. The judge made it clear that if he could've imposed a longer sentence, he would have. Sigg did not get caught with fancy CSI work. He admitted his guilt to his mother and confessed to police. Police released his videotaped confession with certain parts redacted. This video showed him calmly explaining everything that happened and what led him to do what he did. He explained that he had become deeply addicted to pornography. He called himself a monster and said that his addiction escalated until it had to manifest itself in the real world.

The escalating cycle of porn consumption has many potential side effects. Besides a potential relationship collapse, he may lose the ability to perform sexually or maintain a normal sense of sexuality.

"For teens, it becomes a matter of objectification. They start getting in their heads that women aren't equal as human beings. She becomes a sexual object."

—**Craig Lounsbrough, MDiv, LPC**

6

Vitality

THE IP Mistress brings a sense of excitement and joy to his life. She's always excited to see him. She greets him with enthusiasm. She is eager to meet any need she can. If it's not within her capability, she promises to keep trying.

The testosterone boost she causes stimulates his mind, body, and soul. She builds him up through his sexuality. He feels more like a man. With her, he is the star of a sports team. She is the nuclear reactor of his ship, taking up just a small amount of space but generating enough power to fuel activity in all other parts of the ship. The IP Mistress can make him perform better in other areas of his life. He knows that when he needs her energy, he can easily find it. She's always there, doing her job. He may be creating or self-medicating low testosterone.

The IP Mistress makes him feel young and vibrant. A young male is full of energy, hope, passion, and testosterone. Testosterone is what makes him feel more like the man he wants to be reminded of. A young man believes he can do anything. With her, he can. She makes him feel powerful. She makes his mind sharper and more alert. She gives him energy and puts pep in his step. He can display a great and outgoing personality around others because of her. He can even perform at a higher professional level because of her. She makes it easier for him to deal with the pain of life. All pain is either suffered through, managed, or medicated. The IP Mistress is a medication. If he's young, she makes him feel older. As he gets older, she makes him feel like the young stud they both long for. The rush he gets when he reunites with her is intoxicating.

I was having breakfast with a man who was in a middle-of-life collapse due to his pornography consumption. He told me he wanted to get back together with what he referred to as the wife of his youth and quoted a passage from Proverbs 5.

> May your fountain be blessed, and may you rejoice in the wife of your youth. A loving doe, a graceful deer—may her breasts satisfy you always, may you ever be intoxicated with her love.
> **—Proverbs 5:18–19**

The idea of the wife of his youth speaks to passionate young love and connection. The problem today is that many men were introduced to pornography at a very young age, and it became the wife of their youth. This young love held and may still hold deep connection for a man. The wife of his youth was a professional actress being paid to act out the most unnatural type of love and intimacy. She became his first love. His love for her existed prior to his love of his wedded wife. In some cases, his love for the IP Mistress came before his love for God. His arousal template, or sexual preferences, may have been set before meeting his wife or his God. He knew the voice of the IP Mistress before he knew the voice of his wife or God. He learned so-called intimacy from the IP Mistress. If she can come before his God, what chance does the wife have? The guy from the breakfast told me he wanted time to pray about getting help. The IP Mistress *is* the wife of his youth!

7

Victory

NO ONE wants to be a loser—especially your man. The IP Mistress knows this about his spirit. A guy does not mind having to hunt, but it's important that he at least have a chance of catching something. He will invest time and resources in fishing for even the chance of a catch. The buildup can be just as intoxicating as the catch. When he does come away successful, the catch becomes a prize.

Every other relationship in his life is heavy on emotional risk and short on reward. The IP Mistress is all emotional reward with zero emotional risk. Every time he sits down at the slot machine, he hits a jackpot. He gets an endorphin release when he is with her. Endorphins are the body's natural opiate. Artificial opiates like heroin, morphine, codeine, and OxyContin are addictive because they give a sense of euphoria as well as pain relief. He may be self-medicating some sort of physical or emotional pain. Most men have some sort of wound from their boyhood. Commonly, this wound is a father wound. The father may have been absent from the home, absent in the home, abusive, or he may have set such a high bar that the son cannot live up to it. If a man has a past trauma or history of abuse, this can create a nagging internal pain. Pornography can be a form of virtual cutting to replace or mask that pain.

Availability

The IP Mistress understands him. The first way she affirms his need for victory is by *always* making herself available. She also makes the hunt predictable. The formula never changes. She never says no. More specifically, she always says yes. Furthermore, she always says, "Thank you, sir . . . may I have another?" There is extreme power in receiving a "yes" to his desires. Her enthusiastic "Yes!" is what gives her access to deeper parts of his cave. When a porn consumer hears "no" from the woman in his life, it creates an impression of pain in his masculine (though fragile) soul. The echo of the IP Mistress's "Yes!" rings louder in those times.

The London Film School made a film called *He Took His Skin Off for Me*. The video is a very graphic depiction of a man who literally removes his skin for the woman he loves. The result is a new existence for him and consequences for her. Without the IP Mistress, he is no longer comfortable in his own surroundings. The IP Mistress is where she promises to be, and she will always respond to the call. She knows he needs to consume and has an endless supply of what he needs. This is the kind of "hunting" that animals in the zoo are accustomed to. The animals might be wild at heart, but they would be unsuccessful in the wild after growing up in captivity.

Submission

Not only is she always available, but the IP Mistress submits to his victory. She has a submissive nature and gives in to his desires. She understands the power of submission, and there are no limits to her submission to him. She is not subject to the same social stigma around submissiveness to him that his wife must avoid. She understands his tendency to bend toward a spirit of submission.

Many women have been abused, but society teaches women today that weakness and vulnerability must be kept hidden. The masculine nature of most men is drawn toward a heart of vulnerability. This gives him a place to rest his strength. Spiritually and emotionally weak men abuse women, possibly as a way to force them into weakness. Spiritually and emotionally weak women may turn to a man with controlling tendencies to achieve the same result.

The IP Mistress asks him what he wants and does whatever she can to meet his needs. He feels safe opening up his deepest needs to her because she never rejects him. She never puts him down or shames him for his guilty pleasures.

Most broadband-Internet porn consumption leads to some form of violence. The IP Mistress is so submissive that even when she is hurt or abused, she quickly forgives him and comes back for more. Most women cannot, would not, *and should not* submit to this level of violence. I am merely illustrating what the IP Mistress offers. It's an unrealistic level of commitment to a man's victory. He trusts her with his heart because she has proven herself trustworthy.

I can recall a story of a mom who discovered her middle-schooler's porn use on his cell phone. Not only was she shocked to discover this activity, but she was devastated by the graphic and violent nature of the porn her "baby" was consuming. For the first time, young people en masse are being introduced to the most violent and intense forms of pornography right away. In the past, porn was commonly referred to as "soft core" or erotica. These two terms imply sensitivity and love. Now, the predominant types of porn are all referred to as "hard core." This speaks to the heart or nature of the material currently being consumed.

Today's porn makes no attempt to invest in plot, story line, or even specific female porn stars. It has become a factory producing whatever females can do to perform the most unnatural sex acts possible. Now there are increasing stories of actresses having to do drugs just to perform to the extreme levels required today.

8

Vacation

OUR LIVES are full of stress. If you're like most, after you lay your head down at night, you think about your stress. The chronic stress we live in wreaks havoc on us.

One common way to deal with stress is to get away from it. We plan and commit to escaping our daily jobs, yard work, house issues, school, weather, traffic, cooking, cleaning, or anything else we don't fully enjoy. Most do not vacation in their home or neighborhood; it's about the getaway. The IP Mistress is the Hotel California. As in the Eagles song, you can check out, but never leave. She is that place the consumer goes to medicate the effects of stress on his life. She serves him emotionally, spiritually, and physically. She allows him to escape, even though he's escaping to a cold and dark place. Also as in the Hotel California, you can stab it, but you can't kill it.

She does all this for free. How long would the lines for cruises be if Norwegian, Royal Caribbean, or Disney did not charge? The IP Mistress prepares for him, serves him, promises him a good time, entertains him, and even cleans up after him. (OK, that last one may have been too much.) She is the vacation and stress relief he can have almost whenever he wants. This vacation is a metaphor, but the vacation has a chemical component.

Cortisol

Stress is closely tied to the hormone cortisol. Its role is to help us with the fight-or-flight response. This response goes hand-in-hand with the instinctive part of the brain. A spike in cortisol puts him into nearly instant warrior mode. We were not created to be in a constant state of tension. One of the commonly recommended ways to reduce stress is to have sex.

Oxytocin

The perfect chemical antidote to cortisol is oxytocin, which is commonly called the "love drug." It has very powerful effects on our connection to each other. It increases trust, relaxation, and mental stability. Most women experience large oxytocin dumps during and after delivering a baby. To induce labor, doctors give women Pitocin, which is a synthetic version of oxytocin. Oxytocin is spiked in the mother and the child during nursing.

Oxytocin plays a big role in creating sexual bonds between two people and also performs a major role in sex. Not only is it linked to bonding and attachment, but it is also found to increase during orgasm. I speculate that a man's level of sexual commitment increases as he receives steady doses of oxytocin from any source. Maybe he is not interested in attending a marriage conference because it takes him away from who (or what) he's most connected to. While testosterone plays the main role in a male's sexual buildup, oxytocin appears to be a main driver of a woman's arousal.

> Consider: Couples that have regular sex live longer with less disease. We can trace this back to hormones. Frequent sex raises the production of our feel-good hormones, testosterone for men and oxytocin for women. That's just the nature of sex. But when sex is combined with feelings of love and affection, the act triggers an even greater release of these heavenly hormones to lower our stress levels and regenerate our bodies.
> —John Gray, PhD, *Venus on Fire, Mars on Ice,*
> **Mind Publishing, 2010**

Both males and females release oxytocin during sex. When your man releases oxytocin during virtual sex, he begins to create deeper bonds. In November 2013, the Proceedings of the National Academy of Sciences of the United States of America published a study named "Oxytocin: the monogamy hormone?" In the study, married men were given oxytocin and shown pictures of their family. Using brain scans, the men showed less dopamine activity when they were shown pictures of other women.

Yes, I'm saying he creates more connection, trust, and loyalty with whoever, or whatever, he is most sexually tied to. Therefore I recommend guys keep their eyes open during sex with their partner. I also recommend eye contact with his partner during orgasm whenever possible. This is tied to the visualization factor. Humans are the only species anatomically designed for face-to-face sex. This is another example of how we are wired and created for intimacy. Ladies, regardless of how you feel about your own body, *turn on those lights*!

9

Validation

THIS MAY be the most significant benefit he gets from the IP Mistress. Because of this benefit, a tremendously deep connection forms with her. She is the most reliable thing in his life. She never leaves him, and as a result, he is reminded that she is reliable. This is the kind of love and acceptance he has desired his entire life. This is the kind of love and acceptance we all seek.

Women might say they want their man to be completely open and tell them everything. Most men have experienced telling a woman something that makes them somewhat vulnerable only to have it backfire, making them feel judged or rejected afterward. The IP Mistress has a tangible way of reminding him she'll never leave. It takes no faith to see her; she reveals herself at every opportunity. He is tied so deeply to her that he begins to see himself as a captive subject. He identifies himself by her and through her. The IP Mistress is a woman with deep control issues. She exercises her control by constantly asking how she can better meet his sexual needs.

This IP Mistress's identity is a chain of bondage, but it also provides comfort and security. She affirms his every wish. She always tells him he is a good person. She tells him he is the best. She never judges him, and she gives him a sense of security. He may be self-medicating emotional, spiritual, or sexual-identity issues. The more she draws him in, the more she controls him. Her affirmation becomes the air he breathes. This affirmation becomes slavery. Picture this devil not with a pitchfork and horns, but as something beautiful that provides what he really desires. She gives him so much that it destroys him. She understands the idea of mutual submission, and she knows the more she submits to his sexual will, the more he will submit to her call. He surrenders to her, and whatever you surrender to determines your identity. He will believe only what she allows him to believe. He will only be able to get as far away from her as she allows him to. She doesn't even allow him to get a night of sleep away from her. She has the ability to hold his attention for many hours at a time.

He knows her voice better than any voice he has ever known. When she calls him by the name she has given him, his subconscious response is to look. He will see himself as a weak failure with no other choice but to live in this way. The idea of living without her becomes unthinkable. He is terrified at the thought. She is the best medication he has ever known. She might be the *first* medication he has ever known. He knows that she controls him, but he receives this as a form of nurturing. Oxytocin is stimulated as he receives sexual release from her. She was the first to whisper deep into his spirit, telling him, "I will sacrifice my body for you. I will never leave you. I love you unconditionally. I am here to serve you. You are here to serve me. Give me everything you have, and I will give what I have back to you." She can become his god.

She constantly meets his deepest need as if she were a nurturing mother seeking to soothe her crying baby at the breast. Yes, the IP Mistress is ruining his life, but her validation can seem irreplaceable. Freedom is secretly more terrifying than the thought of losing everything he has in her. It is a deeply abusive relationship, and he cannot tell anyone about it because of the shame and fear of being judged. She allows him to live what appears to be a normal life. She knows he is coming home to her. Even when he tries to live without her, she reminds him that she is always willing to again take away all his pain. She's always there with passive-aggressive control.

If he were truthful, he would admit that he trusts the IP Mistress more than his own wife. The path to the husband's heart is through his sexuality. It's not the quantity of sex as much as the depth of his ability to be sexually vulnerable. The wife's lack of trust for the porn-consuming husband is easily understood. The real issue is that he doesn't trust his wife with his most vulnerable places. He cannot trust her to see him with his skin off. He feels that he will be judged and condemned if she really knows him. In some ways, he doesn't love himself and doesn't trust her with his deepest insecurities. Not many wives can handle a tour of his dark cave. His underwear and socks are nothing compared to his cave. The only way she can earn his trust is to find a way to go into his cave and come out without making him feel judged for what he sees. This is understandably difficult, given she might have wounds, trauma, and a lack of trust in him. She won't get the full tour right away.

The IP Mistress made him feel emotionally safe as he revealed more and more over time. With each step she reminded him that she wanted to know him and would not judge him. Once she gained his trust, she set the standard. So can his wife.

I understand this book will make some women feel uncomfortable and challenged beyond reasonable expectation, but imagine how he will feel as he shows you parts of himself he may have never shown anyone except the IP Mistress.

"The cave you fear to enter holds the treasure you seek."
—Joseph Campbell

10

Cycles

LIFE CYCLES are everywhere. Habits are cycles played out in our conscious and subconscious mind. The consumer's Internet porn problem *and solution* follow a series of powerful and continual cycles.

Addiction Cycle

His engagement with the IP Mistress becomes an increasing part of his life. At some point, before he realizes it, his consumption becomes an addiction. This addiction cycle is dangerous.

The stress of covering up his deep pains and insecurities causes high levels of the stress hormone cortisol. The natural tendency is to seek medication, as medicating the pain provides some sort of relief. Porn is a free and unlimited medication. Turning repeatedly to porn makes porn the dominant trap in his life. Through the porn trap and the six Vs, he finds relief in the form of the pain-relieving endorphins. Finding relief from the pain through porn completes the cycle but leads to increased stress and pain.

Addiction Cycle

© RISE Properties, LLC 2015

Medicate Cycle

As he digs deeper into his medication, we will see that his medication becomes a continual cycle. The brain's gas pedal chemical of dopamine drives him to whatever he perceives as necessary for his survival. For him, surviving involves avoiding pain by seeking pleasure. Dopamine floods his brain, causing what becomes an unbearable drive toward a payoff. His teakettle is always sitting on a hot stove. The pressure is constantly building up. At some point, the internal pressure demands a release. When he slips, breaks, or gives in to the urge, the IP Mistress is there for him. After his encounter with her, his payoff is in the form of bond-creating oxytocin. Because she was the source of the payoff, she is yet again affirmed as his answer. This repeated affirmation becomes the addictive habit.

This habit becomes a muscle, and the more it is exercised, the bigger and stronger it gets. DeltaFosB is a brain protein to help solidify the habitual muscle. The stronger the habit muscle, the more it squeezes out dopamine to continue the cycle.

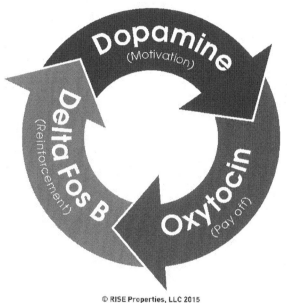

© RISE Properties, LLC 2015

What Pain Is He Medicating?

Given this information, it is easier to see that he is his own pharmacist. I love Dr. Mate's quote, "Instead of asking why the addiction, ask why the pain?" He can now medicate his pain with an internal yet external, free, and unlimited stimulus. The more he depends on the IP Mistress, the more he attaches to her.

My early identity was formed around emotional pain. There is real pain associated with living up to a standard that may or may not be attainable. Add in the pain of being physically, emotionally, or spiritually violated, and I became emotionally and neurologically handicapped. I don't want to make excuses, but these are tangible factors. The only person I could safely bring my pain to was also a main source of my pain. My pain tortured me. So did my medication. I was forced to suffer in silence because of shame, guilt, and stigma.

If your man could just stop on his own, he would.

Freedom Cycle

There is good news! It is possible to get free from these two cycles. Is it easy? No! It is completely possible, though. In my search for answers, I had not heard of anyone with a specific plan on how to do it. I could not find a plan for what to do when I woke up in the morning in this battle. I was able to find information and even inspiration, but not application. This is what led me to develop the answer that I teach and speak about.

The freedom cycle begins with the promise found in Galatians 5:1. It says, "It is for freedom that Christ has set us free. Stand firm, then, and do not let yourselves be burdened again by a yoke of slavery."

To believe that, you must have some level of faith. In my experience, having faith alone is not enough. That is politically and religiously incorrect to say. I have cried on the floor of many men's conferences. I have prayed countless times for God to take porn addiction away from me. I have heard many sermons and talks about how bad porn is and how much of a sin it is.

I was hooked on porn before I was a believer. My sin thermometer was calibrated for porn before I knew what sin was. If believing alone were enough, there wouldn't be pastors hooked on porn. Faith must be applied. James 2:17 says, "In the same way, faith by itself, if it is not accompanied by action, is dead."

You must work on your physical body on a regular basis, strengthening your body in the form of physical exertion. Exercise allows you to naturally stimulate dopamine, endorphins, and norepinephrine. A Duke University study (*Duke Today*, September 22, 2000) showed that thirty minutes of jogging or riding a stationary bike three times a week preceded by a ten-minute warm-up and five-minute cool-down was as effective as taking the antidepressant Zoloft. Cortisol is stored in the muscle. You can also release stress through exercise. Additionally, new brain cells are created through regular exercise.

Once you activate your faith through physical work, you are driven to a place of worship. John 4:24 says, "God is Spirit, and his worshipers must worship in the Spirit and in truth." You must deepen your effort in spiritual worship. This is medicating through intimacy with God and the endorphin release created by deep worship. This is strengthening your soul as opposed to cutting it.

Freedom Cycle
(Gal 5:1)

© RISE Properties, LLC 2015

The cycle is completed with seeking the Word. John 1:1 says, "In the beginning was the Word, and the Word was with God, and the Word was God." You must expand your brain through exercising it. Constantly learning something new should become part of your life. This involves seeking God's word as well as general knowledge and information about anything. Seeking knowledge is how I learned everything that contributed to my class and this book. To free himself, he must be able to drive on new ground and passionately pursue new and deeper ideas.

> *"The learning process builds confidence.*
> *Confidence then builds internal empowerment."*
> —**Stacey Wheeler Slaughter, Owner/CEO, NCTI**

"Just Stop?"

BECAUSE OF pornography, relationships and true intimacy will become extinct. We will need to better solve the problem of reactive attachment disorder. The longtime consumer of free broadband-Internet pornography will develop the inability to connect with people. He trusts no one fully. True intimacy does not exist in his world, and it may never have existed. We are biologically wired for connection with one another. True intimacy is shared brokenness. Soon, the only intimacy that will exist will be virtual in nature. We will only connect with things that spike certain brain chemicals.

Feed the Lion

Have you ever gone to the circus and watched the lion tamers in action? They put on a good show with fancy outfits, whips, and a power they seem to have over many lions at the same time. I've wondered how these trainers have gotten the lions to forget that they are actually higher on the food chain. Surely the animals should be able to sense that they are bigger, stronger, and more powerful than the humans making them perform the tricks. The secret element is that the circus ensures the lions are well fed. The lions never experience hunger, which triggers their animalistic and limbic response. Sometimes you see the trainer throwing bits of meat to the lion as a reward for obedience; thus, the trainer becomes an external limbic system for the lion. Keeping the lion's belly full and continually reminding the animal of the source of its satisfaction are key.

Likewise, for your man to understand his porn problem means he must examine his emotional hunger. This is the beginning of seeking relief from the craving. Porn is his circus. As he tries to move away from pornography, he will look to his spouse for oxytocin and endorphins. Quite often, the spouse is hurt and wounded and cannot bring herself to try to meet his needs. He is used to having the IP Mistress always there. For him to reach out to his wife and then be rejected is emotionally devastating. The man in him is not the one experiencing the rejection, it's the hurt boy who retreats to the cold, dark places. The only one willing to follow him into that dark cave is the IP Mistress. In her hand is a small piece of meat that she tosses in his direction. This is a reminder that she has been the only one to never let him down or reject him. In a perfect world, his wife would understand his problem from the inside and find a way to help feed the lion or at least join him in the cave. At least they can be broken together. Developing a network of other trustworthy men can help him develop the ability to connect on basic levels.

12

IP Mistress Weaknesses

THOUGH EXTREMELY powerful, the IP Mistress has some obvious limitations. She is two-dimensional. We are three-dimensional beings. We have a mind, body, and soul. The IP Mistress is not real. She is literally in a box. Because she is confined, she has limitations. We can exploit her limitations to gain an advantage in understanding and helping him.

Touch

The IP Mistress cannot physically touch him. The obvious exception to this feeling is the masturbation that most certainly accompanies porn consumption. One way to stimulate the release of oxytocin, serotonin, and endorphins is through physical touch. A well-known theory suggests that a six-second hug releases enough of these chemicals to change one's mood. As your man tries to free himself from the IP Mistress's trap, there are few more fundamental ways to help than to physically hug him. Touch is key. If he is trying to gain freedom, you probably cannot touch him too much. Yes, this includes appropriate sexual touching as well as nonsexual touching. Quite honestly, he should get used to your touch in his intimate areas more than his own. Just placing a hand on his thigh when sitting next to each other will go far with him. I know that's pushing it, but I'm still keeping it real.

Nonsexual touch is equally important. Exploring and asking him where else he likes to be touched shows your concern and helps bring down walls of vulnerability and intimacy. Most men like to be touched somewhere above the shoulders. If you're touching him, there is no need for him to seek stimulation elsewhere. Watch professional athletes closely. Even in extremely competitive and often violent circumstances, they physically touch each other after something good or bad happens.

Smell

Since the IP Mistress exists in a box, she does not have a smell. This is significant because, of all our senses, smell is the only one that bypasses brain circuitry and goes straight to the memory. Smell is also our most primitive sense. Smell is tightly associated with the parts of the brain that regulate emotions. Real estate agents place fresh-baked cookies in model homes when you walk through them only for this reason. Everyone responds to that new-car smell.

Smell is extremely powerful in forming deep memories. You can exploit his sense of smell. Plant light traces of perfume to remind him of you at odd times of the day. If you already wear a scent or perfume, be sure he smells it on you, especially during sex. Find a way to send it with him to work or away on a business trip. I would suggest acting quickly before the IP Mistress figures this one out.

Dialogue

The IP Mistress is brilliant at talking to him. She tells him what he wants and needs to hear. What she cannot do is engage in a dialogue with him. Broadband porn videos can never ask him how his day was. They can never talk with him about the things going on in his life; however, he may consume chat-room pornography in which he can have a conversation with someone on the other side of the screen. This conversation used to happen via paid telephone lines. Now, there are people who have a lucrative career doing the same thing face-to-face using broadband Internet. A man can talk in real time and develop virtual relationships with someone on the other side of the world.

The awesome part is that he must pay by the minute or by subscription for this type of interaction. This is awesome because his spouse can turn the tables on the IP Mistress and do the same thing for free! His spouse can create opportunities for one-on-one time in which he can share what his journey is like. His spouse can invite him to dream about goals and aspirations. Exploring his goals and dreams is key, because his soul now needs a purpose. That cup needs to be filled. Obviously, the IP Mistress would never discuss his journey to freedom, so this could begin the process of building intimacy and mutual trust.

Some consideration must be given to the fact that his spouse may not be in a good place to explore her husband's deepest levels of transparency. In fact, the spouse may not be the best person to discuss the deep and heavy stuff, including his past and current pain. This is where a strong counseling routine would be valuable. Another possibility is for him to consult others who are walking through or have walked through the same journey.

Her Chivalry

Genetically, a man is a man because his chromosomes are X and Y. A woman is a woman because her chromosomes are X and X. The woman in his life has twice of what he has half of. Your additional X represents your ability to multiply the relationship to a higher level. That X also represents the variable in his equation. You represent the factor that cannot be fully explained. His Y indicates his natural need for purpose. He has a "why" left unanswered in his natural being. For most men, the woman in his life is and represents his "why." Male literary and film protagonists almost always have a woman as part of their narrative. A man displays his chivalry by doing things like opening doors for her and walking on the curbside of the street to cover her. He needs chivalry from you to open doors to his Y, his heart, his intimacy. He needs your chivalry to safeguard him on the unsafe side of his road to vulnerability and transparency.

The Mistress Spouse

Ladies, I know this world constantly tries to make you think that you are not enough. Whether it's magazines at the checkout line, the fashion industry, movies, television, people closest to you, or even challenges in your career, these things can chip away your worth and self-esteem. Western culture and our "pornified" society have created a standard of objectifying women and valuing only what you can offer for public consumption. The last thing you need is for me to end this book with more of that same message.

Shortly after I began writing this, I realized my target audience will probably be mostly women. Men will not have much difficulty understanding the pictures I'm painting or why porn is such a trap. I am not justifying the behavior. I'm merely explaining it in a way no one else ever has. I want you to understand why the man in your life has this struggle. I believe the good-hearted woman will want to help her good-hearted man as he tries to climb out of the pit. The work is his and all his to do, but you can make or break the odds that he will succeed. You can do more for him than pornography can in the long run. He wants you to meet his deep needs beyond the surface porn issue. He does not know how to communicate those needs to you and probably fears opening up his most sensitive parts to anyone, especially the person who could hurt him the worst. I get that he has hurt you, but hurt people hurt people.

There is nothing wrong with the spouse of a porn consumer becoming his mistress. That doesn't mean you must become his porn star. You can make it easier for him to pursue you. I'm not suggesting you become a porn star. You cannot compete with the IP Mistress. No one can. In most cases, even God does not compete. I'm offering ammunition to help your man as he works his way out. This book is the secret sauce to accessing the power of his sexuality. Sex is not bad—the exploitation of sex is. It will not be easy for either of you. Now you have insight into how the IP Mistress does what she does. You can try to fight back and help him fight back. Before we judge a man's medication, we need to first understand his pain. He doesn't need you to be his porn star; he needs you to love him unconditionally and just try to meet him where his intimacy was stunted. You, as his wife, are the only one chosen to meet certain needs of his. Maybe that is the help your spouse needs from you. He's not as broken as you may assume. He's actually working quite well—just exploited. You, as the woman in his life, can help the rescue operation by giving him a safe place to rest his masculinity and vulnerability. I know I may be asking some of you to do what seems impossible given your experience and wounds. We're asking him to do what seems impossible given his experience and wounds as well. How can we ask him to do something we are not willing to do ourselves? That is overcoming something that has controlled him for most of his life.

Seek to understand him and then work to love him. If you can help him in his journey to freedom, you will discover a warrior inside the wounded. He is desperately seeking deep intimacy and true vulnerability. If he can grow to look to you for that, you will be surprised at the potential of the man you are with. I know I can show him how to get free. He needs help though, and you are the best person to be in his corner.

To the Guys

Fellas, I believe in you. I get it. I get it from the inside out. I've sat across from many guys as they opened up to me about the ups and downs of their life struggle. I explained the diet version of my story in this book. The dark abyss of hopelessness can be suffocating. The reason I want those around you to understand what it's like is because I want to help you. I want to clear the running lane for you so that when the ball is handed to you there is as little as possible between you and the goal line. You can do it. You already have everything you need to do it except the "how." I explained the "why" to the best of my ability here because I am prepared to show you "how." You are a warrior, and the fight gene is already in you or you wouldn't still be here. You would've quit by now if you were weak. It takes tremendous strength to fight the giant you have grown accustomed to fighting.

Freedom is not quitting. That's the main thing you need to keep in mind. Just don't quit. Ever. The shame will try to get you to tap out. The stigma and judgment will dare you not to say something or come forward for help. Throat-punch that fear, and do it anyway. You are far from alone, and as long as my team and I are around, you will never be forgotten. We will be on a search-and-rescue mission for you. The battle may seem insurmountable, but it only takes several strategic small victories. You are closer than you think. The distance between your valley and your mountaintop is shorter than it seems. The woman in your present or future life needs security. Her man's struggle with pornography taps into deep wounds she may have. It surely gives her a sense of insecurity about your relationship. She wants your leadership and strength to help carry the weight she lives with. When young boys never get to become men, young girls are forced to fill the masculine space. The perceived weakness of a man being caught in this trap leaves a woman feeling she might have to carry that burden alone and forever. Your focus must not be to get free for your woman. Get free for *you*, and everything else will work itself out. You must do the work. You are responsible for the change you need. I am here for you. I love you, bro.

Epilogue

Written for and read at my father's funeral.

My father lived a life few of us could even begin to comprehend—from unimaginable turmoil growing up, to the jungles of Vietnam, to feelings of uncertainty and abandonment with the passing of his parents. He faced living in a world that didn't understand him and that he didn't understand. Among all this, he looked at a family that he had created but could not be a part of. He by no means lived a perfect life, but for us to judge him would be to elevate ourselves above our own imperfections in sin.

I sit and wonder why he was sent to earth to be my father. Why he said the things he said and did the things he did to make me laugh and make me cry. I think of all the life lessons he tried to hammer into my head—most of which I blew off at the time. He told me of the growing pains of a world that can be so cruel to so many and about being a *man* no matter what. I think, "Maybe he told me that then just because he wouldn't be here when I am a husband and father." I think of how I have a burning desire to be the best husband and father on earth. Would I have that desire if it weren't for my childhood? I doubt it. Would I be able to accept the way life can be sometimes if it weren't for that? I doubt it.

This in fact is an end to a chapter of my life. I've waited, and now I've exhaled—not from personal relief but from the relief of knowing he is in a world that understands him, where he can finally rest. He doesn't have to look over his shoulder anymore, because God's world has no enemies. From this point, I have to keep spinning with the world. I must acknowledge the fact that life is short and that my day is coming too. I must strive passionately to be the best person I can be each day God gives me. I can't take my family for granted and let the enemy step in to turn me against those whom I love—and who love me. I can't forget the past, but I can't let it keep me from being what God wants me to be.

Till we reach that distant shore and we shed a tear no more, may God give you strength to endure.

Dad, may His peace be with you, till we meet again.

About the Author

KIRK M. SAMUELS is an author, motivator, inspirator, and bona fide porn liberator. He has inspired others to join him by going into the darkest places of a man's life with the purpose of rescuing the captive. He is a gifted speaker and member of Toastmasters International. One would have to work hard to leave a conversation with Kirk without feeling better.

Kirk was born in Washington, DC. He and his brother were raised in the nation's capital, which was also the murder capital of the world at the time. Kirk's father was an addicted Vietnam veteran, in and out of a mental hospital until he died at the age of forty-six. For thirty of the first forty years of his life, Kirk was addicted to pornography. Numerous relationships suffered as a result, and he also lost a military career. For decades, he yearned for something to free him from that trap.

At his lowest point in the struggle, Kirk was ready to end his life. At that hopeless point in his existence, he experienced the most significant of breakthroughs, and he began to piece together information from many different sources to formulate a plan. For the first time in his life, he found a solution, something that worked, and he knew it could not be kept a secret. Realizing it would be of great benefit to others, he created a class, a program called *f.r.e.e. indeed*. This is a score-based, adaptive behavior method specifically targeting Internet pornography consumption. Since that time, many others have duplicated his recipe, allowing them to experience hope and freedom for the first time in their lives. Kirk's real, practical experience makes him uniquely qualified to speak on the difficulties of the trapped porn consumer, offering insights from the inside and out.

For a free fifteen-minute coaching call, contact me at the website or QR code below.

www.kirkmsamuels.com

Resources the Author Recommends

STEP SEVEN

Our Mission:

SHARING JESUS WITH THE ADDICTED.

Our Vision:

A Christ centered vision of freedom strengthened by the leadership skills taught in our small groups, sober living homes and Sabbath morning celebration.

If you are wondering if Step Seven might work for you or a loved one, ask yourself these questions:

Do I or my loved one continue to quit only to start up again?

Am I (or they) tired of being told that they are powerless and hopeless?

Can I (or they) imagine a future free from these challenges?

Can I (or they) at least consider Jesus as my Higher Power?

If the answer is yes, we would like to invite you to contact us. Our only desire is to help you.

For more information:
888-330-1931 / 303-840-0006
contact@stepseven.org
StepSeven.org

Shepherd's Heart
ministry
SHEPHERDS WHO HURT. SOLUTIONS THAT HEAL.

Shepherd's Heart Ministry is a Biblically-based, Christ-centered counseling organization dedicated to providing healing and restoration to pastoral couples, ministry leaders and missionaries who find themselves in crisis due to marriage issues, extreme burnout, moral failure or wounding in the ministry.

Working though a confidential 5-day Intensive model at one of our local or international retreat centers with one of the qualified and trained SHM counselor couples, both husband and wife receive personalized therapy directly relating to their specific issue(s)

SHM also provides Prevention Programs, Seminars, Training, and Conferences conducted in groups that cover a variety of topics to assist those serving in ministry.

At SHM, we are confident that God wants everyone He has called into ministry to walk out their divine calling and to fulfill His purpose and plan. We believe that no failure is too great for God to redeem.

Shepherd's Heart is a faith-based 501(c)3 organization.

Please contact us at:

Shepherd's Heart Ministry
P.O. Box 4808
Parker, CO 80134
303-884-8030
mail@shmministry.com
Or visit us online at: www.shmministry.com

Made in the USA
Columbia, SC
24 March 2019